Violet In Some Places

Cebo Campbell

Not a Cult
Los Angeles, CA

Paperback ISBN 978-1-945649-48-6

Edited by Safia Elhillo
Proofread by Rhiannon McGavin
Cover by Shaun Roberts

Cebo Campbell's *Violet in Some Places* is the recipient of the 2019 Stories Award for Poetry.

For Ella

A note of introduction

Violet in Some Places is a book of conversations with women.

Pick a page and read one piece and it will seem less a poem than a psalm. Read a few, here and there, and the lessons you pick up may feel something like eavesdropping. But if you read the whole of it, from one end to another, it will unravel my life like a loose memoir. Indeed, *Violet* is poems, but it is also memories, semi-autobiographical lessons—a mirror. But most of all, writing this book was my way of memorializing all the words that raised me. This book is broken into four parts: *Before, Girl, After, Woman*, each phase a different time in my life and the different forms the feminine took before me as mother, sister, friend, lover, partner, daughter. This book is for them.

Thank you.

Contents

Before

One

Heaven is a wilderness I can no longer remember. Life distilled in a rage spiraling in the pattern of the universe. All of it *Woman*. Violet flowers, mighty vines, hope up to the height of atoms. What God creates, creates. So God adds death in her soil to make precious what grows. This is where I found Mary. A bud too young to mother her own memories. Too young to warden what eyes, skin, and ears smuggle through the stigma of being. Burdened to stir from darkness a cosmos. She neither called to me, nor her I. But loosed her petals to curl me into her turning. Turning, turning, and turning. Until all that hope finally screamed.

Two

First language is sound. *Miracle*. Thumping and whirring. Which is like the humming of stars. Which is like the throb of notion. Which is like beginning. She wasn't speaking to me. Not to eyes or nose or bone. But to the heat in her ribs warming me into something. *Go on*. Mary says. *Go on*. Of the woman's sound, all that I will ever be is reverb. Never voice.

Only echo.

Three

Birth. Similar. For all I know. To peeking through a telescope. And seeing Jupiter.

Four

You a boy! DeDe said. Spit her words at me. So hard I saw the difference between my blue and her pink. My hightops and her jellies. My recklessness and her restraint. Vigilance braided her hair into rows. Caution kept shadow from her eyes. She smiled at me. Shook her head in the way only older sisters can. And let me play with her dolls.

Five

Granny spanked us with bare hands. Raised high enough to black the sun. Pain and lesson in rhythm. *Didn't...I... Tell...You?* Not anger words. Memory words. Summoned from the earth to burn a backside. *Didn't I tell you?* Hadn't she? There was so much to tell: This is how you learn. This is how you love. This is how you protect. Hush or I'll whip you a callus for joy. *Didn't I tell you* of all the things in between? Rape and rocking chairs. Blood and water lilies. Of all the places God won't go. And all the places God never leaves. Told. In rhythm. Until sand filled her mouth. Until prayer hid her palms. Same palms that pulled babies out of her daughters. And before that pulled cotton from stems. And before that pulled lions by their manes. Palms stronger than words. All the words she'd never live long enough to tell.

Six

Joni said boys can't be pretty. Said boys can't stare long into mirrors and imagine themselves at thirty. Can't wear ruffles or paint their nails or carry Whitney Houston notes in front of people. Can't cross their legs. Can't dance with their hips. Can't play house—*'less it's to sit there and shut up*. Can't drink from a straw, eat fried chicken with a fork, or decline an offer of tobacco. I asked her then what could boys do? She spat her gum on the floor. *Everything else.*

Seven

Bad, Emily said, *lives much longer than good.*

Eight

Mrs. Steele said of me: *you're such a bright child.* Speaking into me Woman Magic. God Talk. Not boy. Not girl. Not smart or fast or funny. Not good or rotten. Not human. *Bright.* Less word than edict. A conjure. *Bright.* Something above and below my skin. The indestructible enemy of limit. Can't clock brightness. Can't break glimmer into wages. Bright knew history. Bright reached into the future. Bright said hello and never goodbye. This is what she taught me. Whether she knew it or not. How to recognize myself in everything that shines.

Nine

I cried into my mother's shirt. Over something I don't know. But knew. Was disappearing.

Ten

Summer's duty is to reveal. This is summer's pact with the devil. Hide and seek. Discover truths by the count of ten. Summer earth is warm on our bare feet. Busy with watermelon rinds and plum seeds drying into tiny brains. *Hide with me*, Tabitha commands, *in the grass*. Heat lived in that grass. Itchweed and dandelion; twitching with bite bugs. So much green. And in it her little white dress enveloped. Taste of fruit on her lips, she kissed me. Church doors creaked shut somewhere. Ashamed we learned psychic things could be handled. That revelation could be found in more places than books. She kissed me again. And again. Until I knew so many things I shouldn't. Old things. Adam's longing. Far away, her father called. They found us. Little white dress skipping away. Into a sky sagging close enough to touch. Close enough to be revealed as made entirely of feathers.

Girl

Eleven

Mothers love their boys. And sisters their brothers. To little boys, love is a beam. Absorbed into their eyes and bellies. Photosynthesized. And answered laughing from their mouths. Simple binary, is love. Until, Girl. Introduced one morning in thousands. Proof the sun can be different. Love transforms into spectrum and the Boy's heart a chandelier. Love kaleidoscopic. Impossible form, distance and color. Glittering gold before rainbow in every direction and in thirteen dimensions. Speckled in orbs and strokes and gloss. Love for Girl is no longer a beam, but a curiosity. An illuminant. *Hi*, says girl. And Boy's heart freckles the ceiling with its glow.

Twelve

I was told that if you like a girl, you bring her flowers. As many as you can hold. All colors. All classes. Grab them with both hands. Wrest their roots from settlement. Tearing, snapping, ripping—bits of soil racing out as if to warn the next. *He bringeth the end.* Ruin flowers by the dozen. You must. All colors. All classes. As many as you can hold. You must. This is what girls like. How girls learn to like you.

Thirteen

Taccara was baptized in a Louisiana creek that did not have a name. All she felt was water go into her ears, she told me, and take away her hearing. Same water blinded her eyes when she tried to open them. And then it was over. Preacher said what God felt like was everything at once. Walking away from me, she said, *nothing is everything too.*

Fourteen

Father's edict: what a man can hold, he can own. My father's hands chopped wood. They pulled wheelbarrows and stirred paint. They sketched ideas in pencil and raised two-by-fours into livable structures. Strong hands to hold most of the world. I watched those hands grip and squeeze Mary's throat. Pin her against a tub of bathwater. Pinch off communication. From her lungs to her brain. Hands strong enough to take hold of God. Hands made to do, not speak. Hands made to act, not tell. Hands made to rear, not teach. Strong. But not strong enough. *Go on, son.* And take this lesson with you always.

Fifteen

Stonewash jeans cut into shorts. Fraying in soft strands over softer thighs. Drinking pineapple soda from cans. Hair pigtailed in yellow ties. Wrists bound in yellow bracelets. Spirit like a yellow kite. Laughing with their mouths so loud it dims the sun. So loud it shames the angels. White shirts dirty from sweat and candy. White shoes dirty from chasing boys. White teeth shining like a lie. *Let's play a game*, one says, *Truth or Dare.* I suffocate my thoughts. No one dare. Tell the truth.

Sixteen

We found them in the fields. Young bodies browning under June sun. Lazed and giggling. Air between them sweetened with the smell of dates. We hid in the palms. Ears tilted towards their lessons. Sometimes their laughter arrives with the breeze. To draft our dreams into the pilgrimage of clouds. They were, to us, like fallen dates. Golden forms, swollen with life. And we were the grass. Upright appetites obsessed with the day. Longing for it to fall from the heavens and lie in our midst. One of them sees us. *What y'all want?* We run away. Fast as we can. Because we don't know the answer. Just the want. No more than the grass can articulate why it longs for the sun.

Seventeen

I've felt it. And it is better without words. As often better things are.

Eighteen

Mesha took care in folding her love letter. A single sheet. Puffed with her being. She folded her coy into a pleat. Giggling she tucked under, one edge atop another, slightly misaligned. Reversed was her heart, folded with space enough to rip it open. Fears were squashed and folded as petals. Fragile now, a trigger looped in to be inseparable from the heart. It came together like an ask. To be unraveled. All that remained of her was stuffed like feathers between the words. A kiss in lip gloss. A spray of her mother's perfume. For my eyes only. So much of who she'd been and who she'd become. Energizing the ink. Goosing the paper. A girl unraveling into my lap.

Nineteen

No one is whole. Made well, many, but none whole. Burdened are human days in pursuit of our parts. I found Lynne under a Ferris Wheel. Her youth expressed itself in pout and mispronounced words. In rainbow socks and a pocket full of tokens. The sun sank into twilight. Stars thumped holes into a purpling sky. A moon rind dodged carnival lights and laughter shot up in beams. Joyous clicking, twirling, screaming—what feels like all the colors glowing at once. A universe broken into pieces. And more pieces. Until only a memory of completion remains. She needn't say anything. Not her. Not Lynne. The piece I knew I was missing.

Twenty

Sudden. Lust is. But long in waiting. Like a bullet from a gun locked in my father's chest since the day I was born. Before then, perhaps. Resting in wait. Since the day Adam woke to his first sun. Outside of Eden.

Twenty-One

I call Elisa while my mother sleeps. *Hi,* she says, like a match struck in the dark. Sound and smoke spiraling out for a surface to contact. Tender egos liberated from tongues. *Hey,* I say, and witness language become gravity. Because all that makes up gravity is knowing. And we don't know anything except how to want. And to soften collisions with flesh. Turn the lights off. Listen to the sound of innocence. The noise above mountains and under trees. Noise from the moon who reflects and suspends. *You hang up first.* She says. Hang up. Suspend us on a Grecian urn as we are too young to count days by the sun. Too young to neglect the dreams of molecules. Let's make atoms of our hearts and send them through coiling wires. Like a door to some other dimension. Where teenage Gods play life in the dark.

Twenty-Two

Even so young. I knew. It pleased them all. To have my attention.

Twenty-Three

I took off my clothes because she drove a Honda and smoked joints out in the open. You see, Selena never laughed at funny things. A raw magic. Made of looks in lieu of spells. Fear in contrast to wonder. Zombies are what they called the boys doing her schoolwork. See, because even dead eyes can marvel. With their hearts wedged in trees. Just to be wounded. Her smile opened up like a wound. Like a cut of moon revealed by the movement of clouds—I see you, daughter to the Mother of Nine. Terrifying voodoo red. Which is violet in some places, pink in others. *Be still*, she says, *be still.* I do what she asks. Because the rings on her fingers resemble tentacles and her mouth the ocean. It feels like dying, so I've heard. And I am afraid to die. But somewhere in her breathing I hear Oshun. And I know death cannot be this warm. This is no place for penance. Nor some box to swallow confession. This is an altar made to conjure a brightness. So, I cover my eyes with both my hands. Conjure all that violet. And try to imagine what it feels like to be born.

After

Twenty-Four

If you stare long enough at the ocean, you will lose count of the waves. And the amount of land taken from beneath you. *So what*, Mandy says, *everyone loses their virginity*. I look up and try to trace a cloud's origin back to a single Pacific whitecap. Ocean is the keeper of change and I have never been nor will I ever be safe from it. A gift that takes. Absconding the body mass of being and becoming. You learn to find joy remembering things you could never forget. Learn to neglect a million waves and bits of sand. Count them all if you wish. The ocean will never say what all that loss makes you. But whatever you've become, eventually you will lose that too.

Twenty-Five

It is by good deeds that little boys become wretched men. We worship grimaced chins. We call ourselves heroes and assign our ambitions to valor. We order first. Put crests on our names in the symbol of animals. Swing hide coats over mud puddles and hold doors. Wood and bone and rock. Condemn the sin of softness. Use your hands. Tear the violets from your heart. Be stronger than your tears. But you can't. And will never be. *It's alright*, she'll say, *it's alright*. And this will be the lesson of strength.

Twenty-Six

I know Lauren felt their eyes. Holding onto her like ropes lassoed from cowboys at whom I was never allowed to look. She asked if I was afraid to hold her hand. We toured the boardwalk. Her yellow hair made yarn of sunlight, her blue eyes turned ocean into droplets. *I don't care what they think*, she said. But I did. I cared that the sun shined on her skin and burned inside mine. That the ocean found a cousin in her eyes and drowned my family. I cared that the lassos came to her as a rescue and to me as a noose. We walked to the end where her father waited next to a station wagon. She waved goodbye. Her fingers scraping quietly against the sky. Quiet as clouds. Quiet as hope. Nearby, someone whispered nigger so sharply it echoed.

Twenty-Seven

If you only knew how often the light says you belong to me.

Twenty-Eight

Under the pier, moonlight painted a likeness in our skin the daylight burned to erase. *This is just between us*, she said, *and just for tonight.* She wore her rosary and a skirt with a school crest. Her heart beat in her wrists. *Church was in revival*, she said, *and all Pastor talked about was dying.* We were fifteen. Too young to think about dying. Old enough to play at living. *God knows everything*, she told me. And something about how it didn't matter anyway. Besides me and God, only things never seen again knew the delights along the roof of her mouth.

Twenty-Nine

My friends said pretty girls stay home. *I'd rather be alone*, Lena said. When they could, my friends asked her things like, *What are you?* Because Manila shaped her eyes and Trinidad her throat and Wales strapped a board in her posture. Exotic. And somehow exotic meant liable. At the parks, grown men walked by her the same way they peeked into lit windows. Shouting stains into innocent lexicon: sexy, pussy, whore. New language for newer discoveries. For a life in imitation. *I ain't ever gonna have kids*, she said. *'Cause they'll never see the sun*. She shut the door and pulled the shades. On the hottest day of summer.

Thirty

We were always in the woods. Looking for fairies or gnomes or sparkling things to confirm miracles age bluffed out of our bodies. Zephyr raised her hands up like antennae. *I can feel it*, she said, *can't y'all?* It was October and the air burned sweetly through gathered chill. She closed her eyes. Her skin listened. Her feet drew power from the ground. The silence felt like a communion. One I could not attend. Twin to the flowers. Breathing sun. I think we all knew what we gave her. Because we knew she was the only one strong enough. So when they found her body floating in the bay, we understood the sea's call to martyr. We grew up and she stayed young. To keep for us the light age would otherwise take. All of it gold and warm and unknowable. A flower. Floating on an ocean without a floor.

Thirty-One

Some days. I feel myself saying sorry. To no one. And everyone at once.

Thirty-Two

Afterwards, I didn't know how to leave. Too young yet to make a lesson of sin. Tisha said of this only: *You're wrong*, and I believed her. The window was still open and her mother had an hour left on her shift. Tisha cradled the pillow up to her chin. And I imagined trying to comfort a carcass. I imagined being confirmed in some prophecy she'd been warned to sense. Wives' tales told by wives who knew better. But I couldn't hear the words steaming off her body. Only want like a bee humming, fruiting fury bitter enough to eat itself alive. I didn't know how to leave. So I washed my hands and imagined God glancing away. Busy tending Saturn. Busy breathing clouds. Busy sanding beaches. And I swore to remember Tisha's eyes the color of acorns. I swore. But in years recalled only how difficult a father's sins are to seed. I didn't know how to leave. But left. Back to the daylight, back to the world: enlisted in the band of men who never learned to stay.

Thirty-Three

Caroline walked barefoot to be closer to the earth. Less in ritual than in apology. She owed a debt to her childhood. To the seasons. To the fast-moving bees. To grounded leaves golden dead. To the dew beading lily petals. To the ice and stone piling into mountains. To her grandmother's lessons that became her mother's, that became hers. To how easily she forgot. To the horses outside her window that stirred in the night, and grew horns in her dreams. To the storms that frightened her, purpling the sky until fear swelled into poetry. To the oak trees with trunks like her dead father's chest. To losing the ability to hear his voice in the woods.

Thirty-Four

Kelly bled down her legs. *Every month*, she said. Her mother called it a cycle sometimes, and other times a period. I'd no mind to figure being two things at once. How to be bleeding and living. No mind to figure girl in transition still woman fulfilled. Binary in multitudes. "Does it hurt?" I ask. She answers even with words swollen in her cheeks. I'd no mind to understand pain stretched over a lifetime nor as steam at the base in every breath. Two things at once. I imagine the moon combing back the sea, until the sun impels return and that somehow this is girl and woman, daughter and sister—child of the moon gleaming like something the sun made. Bleeding and living. Tender enough to bow an ocean, strong enough to strain the seams of a planet. As vulnerable and knowing as the bulb of the eye. I see you now. And know which God to worship. But I'd no mind to understand towers raised in earnest erect summits from which to fall.

Thirty-Five

Mercy, Ruth said, as if my love was punishment. Mercy as if every step in my direction was of feet bare atop glass. *Mercy*, Ruth said, as if future destruction flashed in the present; the end of the world prophesied by touch. Mercy as a conjure of spell against spell: burn the earth to stop love from latching. *Mercy*, Ruth said, as if a sickness filled her mouth with the taste of melon. Mercy, spoken loud to anyone's god: there's a boy playing at the guillotine, and a heart beating in the trap. *Mercy. Mercy. Mercy.*

Thirty-Six

On a magazine cover, I looked for my mother. Black woman: chin jutted forward like a seaboat sure of course. A lighthouse in her chest. The faces shining back don't resemble Mary. Vogue, I see, Marie Claire, Elle. Art-directed pouts, not sorrow made sweet. Not joy so heavy it sags. Not like my mother. But a mimic of innocence and all I'd known of magic manufactured. Dormant is beauty without love. Dormant is love without toil. There is no toil in these flowers enough to say: *The Most Beautiful Women in the World.* They do not look like my mother. So I learn in those aisles the ease with which lies become law. And my sisters, behind me, learn the parts of themselves to disfigure.

Thirty-Seven

What I am going to teach you, said Jackie, *time will appreciate.* A lesson in body words. Cuneiform in quivers; language in the power of muscle and the placement of tongue. *All the way in*, she says, *until everything is gone.* Heavy were her years on me. Wisdom steaming off flesh and shadow. There were no straight lines in her classroom. But shores and mountains and glittering pools warmed by the transmutation of sunlight. Oh woman. Oh god. Praise the splendor of soul hardened into body weight. Hold on to me. Listen for your sermon. Use your fingertips in the steam to pen your name and lay claim. Yours. Until violet ripens behind your eyes. Until blindness makes warmth. There is no magic. Just labor. A tillage upon which a good man learns to rebuild Eden. With all his heart and shoulders and hands. Pushing. Sinking. Saturating. All the way in. Taking his course in pleasure. *Come on*, she says, *you'll know when you've made it.*

Thirty-Eight

Don't take it personally, Katie said. *On TV every man I've ever seen. The ones worth loving. Don't look nothing like you.*

Thirty-Nine

Saturn, she told me, *has sixty-two moons. And Jupiter closer to eighty*. Satellites. Touring more in allegiance than love. Broken shards. Reminders of how easily a thing can end. *Earth only has one moon*. For better or worse. Not a portion, but a parallel. A need amid wants. A give and take. To lose each other would mean the end of the world. And everything on it. So they tell me, this is what it is supposed to be like. And this is what I know it isn't.

Forty

Love as a debt matured since womb. Life payable to the God I failed to serve. Love as an accumulation. A wretchedness to be cleansed. Love as an engine in my bones made entirely of appetite. Love as consumption. A craving to the edge of glutton. Love as a balance overdue. Red in my mother's ledger. Cotton in my sister's penny jar. Love as a know- better. Love as a get-back. Accrued by what the body thinks it knows and persuades the soul to forget. Love as a shame bearing flowers. Lovely, beautiful flowers. I owe you. All of you. And you most of all. So I carry my mother's weight to the altar. *I ~~am~~ due.*

Forty-One

What satisfies the appetite of a man? Not industry. Nor land. Nor oceans. Nor stars. Nor contracts expired by death. Not even love. A man satisfied is a man wanting enough to eat himself alive.

Forty-Two

More than anything. I am sorry. That only broken did I learn the value of my promise.

Forty-Three

Annie and her yellow. Jamaica yellow, as vibrant as joy howled at the edge of the ocean. Yellow-rimmed waves sojourned from Sierra Leone. Talking in laughter. A blinding yellow. Which is sometimes blue. Which is sometimes violet. Which rings out like notes from a steelpan. Preaching love as a cure. Love as the shine. Love as the lemon-colored salt-water stinging into old wounds. Love as impossible yellow. So bright it opens new eyes. And blinds old ones. She says: *keep smiling baby, everything is going to be amazing.*

Forty-Four

It is possible, I've learned. To love the life. And not the person.

Forty-Five

Selene did not believe in God and always paid in cash. Tattoos yet scarred scriptures on her sole. From a place called Farewell. Or Goodbye, though I don't believe anyone can say for sure. Memories stuck in tar. She preferred silence over common words. Spoken from places constellations are most visible. She pulled on a bottle of Jameson with more confidence than I ever imagined possible. She told me about hitchhiking Cusco and how a boy showed her alien remains and how those remains resembled her mother's. Oaths are hard in her mouth. Never does she talk about joy. Nor happiness. Nor love. *Because people are too eager*, she says, *to ruin beautiful.*

Forty-Six

Only at the zoo, among the animals, awed by giraffe and lion and the taste of earth in your mouth—in a tamed wild, had I ever heard you speak of Africa. Or any past or future. With me in it.

Forty-Seven

Every man is pregnant. With every day of his life.

Forty-Eight

I wonder at who teaches a man his lessons. Specifically, the lessons under rule of mysterious ways: God, they tell me, who requires error be learned by commitment. But that error makes stains that can't be washed. *She called me sir.* And something old made a welt I can't say I knew better than to scratch. The ignorance of a boy aged into a man's torment. And a woman's chains. Who will teach otherwise? God? Not the one says evil stirs underfoot. A father is not responsible for what a son doesn't learn. And the agony in his errors are not that boy's own. But his mother's. And his sister's. And his daughter's. By and by. Who will teach otherwise? God? Not the one says sorry will do. Go on, son. And take this lesson with you always.

Forty-Nine

Nia asked, *Have you ever seen a whale?* She didn't mean the ones in bondage, imprisoned by smiles on all sides. And not those poor bones suspended in galleries like wanton chandeliers. *Have you ever seen a real whale? Up close? In the sea?* You can't have. From neither where you stand now nor where you've been would you be so lucky. To do so, you'd first have to leave. Leave behind city sidewalks and veggie burgers and the lonely wrinkles in your bed. Leave days rationed in hours. Leave the comfort of all your knowing. Leave. Go. Until your hands dry. Until a blister forms someplace holy. Until mountain becomes tide. Until time breeds barnacles above your teeth. Until you find yourself beyond yourself. That sea. Unknowable deep. Sinking you into doom on all sides. As dark a blue as death. For what do the heavens matter to something blind to the stars? Your words will cede power. Can't stand. Can't smell. Can't speak. Only feel yourself alive in a constant state of drowning. Suspended in an immensity. And then it will come. Like a truth from nothing made solid. Like impossible gliding in time. Like all you've ever lost returned to you. A majesty larger than dreams. Drifting like a heaven taken for granted. Proof that magic was a patron at the bed of your creation and the ferry to port your burial. You'll look upon it with wonder. Helpless and hope-filled. Animal and spirit. So far and so sudden to learn how to be alive. But you've never seen a whale. So how could you possibly know what love feels like?

Fifty

Lust. Is a blister. From another life.

Fifty-One

In a tuxedo, daughter, one day a boy will arrive at my door. Flowers suspended near his heart. Ella, he will ask for you by name in far too familiar a manner for a boy who doesn't know. He won't know colic screamed you into this world loud enough to wake my heart. Or nights my chest warmed your sleep until you learned to dream. He won't know the peaches I fed you, liquified in tiny jars. Nor the patterns of our foremothers I braided in your hair. He won't know how the ocean smelled where I walked with you at night, until you became indistinguishable from the moon. He won't know how you talked of Paris before you penned your own name. And the shame I feel for not yet taking you. You are more powerful than you are symmetrical. And more curious than you are graceful. He may know you have my eyes. But he won't know that I never taught you to pray. As I saw nothing above you to which you could. I never understood woman until one grew out of my hopes. So he can never truly know the path I cut from my heart to make a better way for you. And still, your freedom scares me the most. This boy will fancy himself a knight in rescue, but he won't know that you saved me. And if he were to ever be so lucky you'd save him too. Come to the door, my love. Let him imagine universes in your voice. Teach him how to hear your unstruck sound. And show him how every vibration of my life, and all the lives of my line, make up the herald that plays your song. I sure hope that boy can hear it. I sure hope that boy can hear it.

Fifty-Two

A man's hands are made as they are meant. They don't change. Bellies change. And cheekbones. And voices. But hands are made complete. Capable of doing and of being responsible for what has been done. Identity affirmed in a print. A future proclaimed in palm. *Take care then*, she said, *of what your hands bring into and take out of this world.*

Fifty-Three

A husband and a father. But not a man. Walking upright on two legs. Big, home-building hands. A voice that booms. A walk like thunder. But not a man. And no man around to teach me how to be one.

Fifty-Four

You learn quickly that it is not a temple. Never was. At your feet you'll see no flowers lain in worship. Only the appraisal of what's most precious. By logos made to look like faces. And hearts dried into ledgers. *Eat the flesh. Drink the blood.* This is what you learn about your body. A threshold too often trespassed. Spiritual sagging. Doing all it can to keep from surrendering. Barely holding anything from getting in. And not letting anything get out. That's all a temple does anyway. Make prisons for gods.

Woman

Fifty-Five

No one. Owns your body.

Fifty-Six

I do not know when a girl becomes a woman. By some moon, I suppose, selected at the sunrise of knowing. To call from coy, woman. Like stars from galactic soot. A something from a nothing. An always from a never. A yes from an impossible. As if an ending wasn't a beginning. Old gods sewing new ones. From and into the material of being.

Fifty-Seven

Mary was the first woman, but not the last. To put clay in my making.

Fifty-Eight

I have tried many times to cook for myself. Greens. Cornbread. Fried chicken. Tried to bring into my kitchen all my mother taught me. And what I could learn from stitch-bound books—clear about how it should go. A little this. A little that. But it's never right. Always feels to be missing something. *Love*, my mother says. *It's missing love. You gotta put passion into it.* But when I mind my cupboard. It shames me to find. This is an ingredient I do not have.

Fifty-Nine

Olivia removes her jewelry one item at a time. Rings first; fingers liberated of gleaming bonds surrendered on a nightstand. Her wedding ring flashes under lamplight. Her necklace, slides down the shadows of her chest. Bracelets take time, as she must undo her right wrist with off hand. Last are the earrings and the anklet she places in the pile of silver and gold. Colloquial etiquettes. *Free*, she sighs. Finally. To do something she will regret.

Sixty

No doubt. Had I my insides under similar siege. I would set fire to the whole system. Just to set myself free.

Sixty-One

Water. Woman. Fountain to life. An ocean makes no claim but of itself. Ancient fathoms deeper than need. For air. For light. For love. Shores like the curvature of suffering. In waves, does sacrifice recur. Even as a taming trespasses on all sides. But flags cannot be raised on water. Her limits are neither names nor the narrow space between continents. She tends the night. Worshipped by the moon. Who dare question the vulnerability of a puddle? Of a river? Of an ocean? *Man. Land.* Born from bodies of water. Teeming with things looking to stake claim. Raising mountains out of rage. Huddling cities into forests set by ceremony to the sun. In the end, we have made all effort to ruin our mothers. But my tears haven't forgotten. We were all water once, and shall be again. A force still pulls me to the coast. I know this. Land can choose to gather dew in comfort of a petal and grow trees with a heart to flower. Land does not understand water. And I do not understand you. But for my part in what has been taken, I'm sorry. To place blame on my father is to place blame on me.

Sixty-Two

I never called after. As a Black man, Lisa said,
how do you not know better?

Sixty-Three

She said: *What right do you have to be you? When you ain't lived a day in your life? Just a bunch of words and walking that's waiting to stop.* All men are kings, I told her. At least, that is what I was taught. Greater kings, some, lesser others. The ransom for our royalty is neither land nor riches, but the subject: woman. She laughed. So loud it shook the clouds. *Ain't no kings, she said, just animals calling perversion religion. And fears laws. All of you. Just boys pretending to be their fathers. What this world would be. I wonder? If more little boys. Pretended to be their mothers.*

Sixty-Four

I am more interested in the mistakes you've made. Not your height. Not your salary. Not your accolades. But in the terrors that rose up to break you. And if your parts found the secret to putting themselves back together.

Sixty-Five

Mary was barely fifty when my stepfather stopped breathing. Through grief I imagined her alone until they reunited. No more going on dates. *No.* No lipstick and worrying over how she smelled. *No.* No pickup at 7. No ordering wine and appetizers. No revealing herself in incremental pieces across a private table. White linen and candles. Carnal thoughts filtered in coy. No longing for the burn of the sun. Not at her age. *No.* I couldn't see her. Not beyond the celebration of youth. In our time. Not when disgust dishonors getting on. The perfect beauty of aging. *No.* Not now. Deceived are both age and beauty. In our time. Where trees need pluck their leaves and pull meat from their trunks. Peel back bark. Withdraw good shade. And feel shame for a closeness to the sun.

Sixty-Six

Winter takes the wildness from a man. Calls it in to hibernate, she said. If any man retains it after snow erases the land. He will go mad. And turn the worst of his kind.

Sixty-Seven

You say *if*, the same way you say *love*. Like jewelry a cigarette dangles from your lip. I can see it now. Sure as the morning. You never wanted happiness. You wanted belonging.

Sixty-Eight

I promised to give you everything. Except everything wild and everything free.

Sixty-Nine

Don't go burying yourself into my skin. Like some secret. Instead. Lay your body on top of mine. Let's love like layers of sediment. Love like the creation of mountains.

Seventy

Her name is Riot. With dreads like roots to the beginning of the earth. Carrying salt in her pockets. Talking that God talk. Magic blowing out of her nostrils. Urgent to be free. Fury visible in her eyes reflecting living memory. Like glimmers of light from the bottom of a well. Or a storm beginning to crack. She calls love a word used too soon and too often. Walks with suffrage in her skin the color of space. Confident only that civility is her enemy. Which teaches men to make words out of their hides. And put barcodes on vaginas. Whore, they call her. Slut. One damned straight to hell. And she wonders what it must be like to walk on the surface of Saturn. Or Jupiter. Or any body suspended in the heavens they worship. *Like hell* but in a state sovereign. Like whore as proclamation of a goddess. Like Mami Wata flooding her own world. Just to save it.

Seventy-One

What will it take? To salvage what I've been taught to suppress? And redefine all the things. I've learned to call by a different name.

Seventy-Two

And suddenly you are lonely. For something you lost. And never knew you had.

Seventy-Three

A black net tends Shirley's hair and her hands the three children chewing breakfast on the train. From ages sixteen down to stroller. They have Shirley's eyes, all of them, but not her nose. Not her lips or chin. But they radiate the same shine now embers in her chest. *Sit still*, to the eldest, wearing headphones that blur the message. Her glare sends other messages too. Speaking to the knowing in their bones and in the dampness under their tongues. This reminds me of Egypt somehow. Of a royalty man can neither give nor take away. One bleached and watered ages can't wash out. Noble are her children. And she is the unknowing queen of all the sand under her feet. I bow in offering she never sees, as I exit the train at 42nd.

Seventy-Four

Right now I am remembering you.

Seventy-Five

I question a machine that requires for its functions the tool of gender. Man. Woman. Boy. Girl. Male. Female. Compartmentalization of the being: human. Of being human. Crack the uniqueness of gender. I question the duty of such a machine. And who in the world hated our unity enough to build it.

Seventy-Six

May aborted her baby. *I know*, she said, *because my body knows.* Because the mind knows. Because the earth knows. Because the stars know. And before good and bad, before right and wrong, the dust knew. That when the time came. She'd be strong enough to decide. For all of us.

Seventy-Seven

We began as. Are. And always will be. An *us*.

Seventy-Eight

You go about your life, Riann said, *and suddenly cross paths with a stranger you feel you already know*. I wanted to tell her about the universe. To say: see that babe—binary in multitudes. We are not the result of happenstance, love, but longing. Go back to when stillness burst fractals. You'll find our pieces. Elemental bits. Traversing some monumental orbit. Hello, dear. Draw close to me in cycles. Magnetism in glittering ratios. See, I hear Fibonacci in your laughter. And I needn't know the whole to know the parts when they orbit back to me. And away again. Planets in rotation. Longing, in all that vastness, to be remembered. Hello, dear. Now is a reminder, I believe, that one day these bones will be trees. And those trees will be tides. And that tide will froth familiarity through its foam. Entangled, are you and I, in all the ways I can imagine. See how your freckles resemble Taurus? And that glance, childhood summers? Settle me by touch as Saturn in transit. Longing and longing and longing to be remembered. And I remember you. Because among constellations of planets and particles in motion, you remain remarkable matter. Hello, dear. It's so lovely to meet you again.

Seventy-Nine

At a certain depth. Water begins to purr. A sound so lovely. You forget you're drowning.

Eighty

Cypress is what I think of. Or Tupelo. Woman of the woods. Lower body soaked in bayou water. Veins that reach down to the beginning of the world. Hair curling out in branches with leaves that chew up the sun. Feel everything. Cut runes out of your skin. Pluck divination from your eyelids. You are connected to a system from which you cannot stray. Not too far, daughter to the moon. Magic is a violet crown above your head. Memory is a weight on your bones. *Remember.* All the power that lives beneath the trees. And what was hung from their branches. Water and root still make conversation. About going far enough back to when everything was a seed. When words were not as strong as meaning. The tide rises. Keep steady. *Remember.* She says. *Remember.*

Eighty-One

My grandmother does not remember my face.

Eighty-Two

Ignorance is not a declaration of innocence. Yet my thoughts mock my throat. How can I be responsible for what I don't know? And how, living these many years, have I always been?

Eighty-Three

In particular, Black woman. Robbed. Of crown. Of soil. Of animal. Of time. Of a connection to Africa's magic. Until memory is just a darkness filled with eyes. How do I help you get back all that was taken? We need you. All of us. To again call spirits from flames.

Eighty-Four

History is proof. At some point, I will fail you. What shames me. Is that, as do I, you've come to expect it too.

Eighty-Five

She called herself damaged. And I imagined a trumpet without a mouthpiece. Broken for duty. Mad to make sounds it couldn't. She didn't understand when I told her she wasn't an instrument at all. Or even sound. But the indestructible place from which music comes. *Be quiet*, she said. And put Coltrane's record on.

Eighty-Six

I've learned. Three-dimensional beings, tangled and sweating, in the dark mapping their bodies to pleasure. Does not make love. *Hold on to me.* She said. *And just breathe.*

Eighty-Seven

Every morning, my love writes the meaning of life on her palm. Lets the day wear it off. There is no magic in that. Just a person. Making their way from one end of living to the other. Understood, from time to time, by a faraway sense of the cosmos.

Eighty-Eight

Woman. I refuse to serve the army. That stands in your way.

Endnotes

As a child, I read poetry only by the barrel of the gun. My professors had to threaten me with failure both in class and in life if I didn't step into what to me was a labyrinth of words out to make me feel, among other things, stupid. Every stanza I didn't understand only confirmed that I did not possess the mind to get to the meaning. It took years before I knew better. I read. But, in truth, I looked forward to the Cliffsnotes after my reading. They helped, like light in the dark, offering clarity and understanding to which I was otherwise blind. Over time, I got better. Over time, the labyrinth of words became less a punishment and more a place of safety. Over time, I grew to love poetry because it granted me something I never expected: *empathy*. Poetry, I believe, is the closest thing in this world to telepathy. Our thoughts are a wilderness of ideas and images and sounds and associations that simply saying "I love you" or "I am scared" fails to express meaning and, moreover, extend with clarity our thoughts to someone else. There is more to words. So much more. And the function of poetry is less to confuse us with them than unite us. Poetry allows us that luscious glimpse into the labyrinth of someone's thoughts so we might understand them, and in many ways, understand ourselves. That understanding makes the world a far more empathetic place. I know that now. Even still, reading poetry isn't easy. I always enjoyed it when an author could offer their thoughts on their own work. They may see it one way and me another, but it helped. So I swore if I ever wrote a book of poems I'd do the same. These are my thoughts.

Before

One

I've always imagined heaven as a great forest, and creation (feminine) a sort of deathless wild. Stuff just growing utterly untamed. I imagine flowers drawing energy into the soil of life—consciousness choosing a mother to bring it into the world. My mother is Mary, and I suppose I chose Mary, whether she was ready or not.

Two

A poem about being in the womb and hearing sound. That sound is a vibration that makes a person. It is like magic, in a way, a spell. All I will ever be is a continued reverberation of that sound.

Three

A poem about being born.

Four

DeDe is my sister. She was the first one to make known a difference between boy and girl, and the society determined to define those differences before you can define them for yourself.

Five

My great grandmother's name was Zinnie. A hard woman, descendent of the Gullah Geechee and Cherokee, who lived through genocide, slavery, rape, Jim Crow—lived long enough to babysit me and my brothers/sisters while my mother worked as a cook. She spanked us almost every day. Sometimes, it seemed, just for breathing the wrong way. As a kid, I thought she was just mean. But, she had so much to tell us that she couldn't. So much she didn't want to get lost in age and forgotten with time. She taught us our place in the world. Where we came from. How we got there. And what we should carry with us as we go on. She beat our backs so we would never forget the forgotten backs upon which we stood.

Six
In school, Joni was always mean to me. I remember she hit me and I hit her back. Trouble, that was. Never do that. Never hit a girl. But why, I asked, when she hit me? Her answer taught me, in that moment, more than school ever had.

Seven
A poem about stains. They can be seen as a blemish on a perfectly white canvas. Or a stroke on a work of art. You'll do bad things. You will. And, you have to know it will be okay. This is what Emily taught me.

Eight
Mrs. Steele is one of my dearest friends and mentors to this day. Her words changed me. To call a child "Bright" is to make them a light, beyond all the definition the world looks to settle upon us. She called me bright, and it set me free.

Nine
A poem about how youth unravels away from us. A closeness to our mother unravels away from us. A

memory of being in that wilderness of heaven unravels away from us. We feel it. Even as children. And spend the rest of our lives, I think, trying to find it again.

Ten
A poem about my first kiss. This was when I began to feel wants I didn't understand. This is when I sensed that losing one connection (mother) meant searching for others.

Girls

Eleven
Lord, girls used to make me so nervous. The nerves felt like something glowing inside me. Something dormant, otherwise, unless activated by the possibility of love.

Twelve
I think the idea of affection being tied to some almost violent act is taught to us early. But to love, time reveals, is a softness. Affection is delivery of that softness, even when the love is tough.

Thirteen
I was a deeply Christian kid. One could be no less growing up in the American South. I do not belittle anyone's belief, however misguided, but I've always found it astonishingly oppressive what religion shackles upon the woman and her body. I sensed that even at an early age.

Fourteen
My biological father beat my mother. I remember being woken in the middle of the night to hide from him in the neighboring park while he patrolled, drunken and mad,

looking for my mother. A boy cannot look up to a man who beats his mother—the closest thing he knows to God. She showed me she was stronger than his anger. Stronger than I could ever imagine.

Sixteen
Near my grandmother's house was a field and on it grew plum and pear trees, an enormous pecan tree, and, at each corner of the field, date palms. We played football in that field and hide and seek, and on summer days we just lay in the heat and watched the clouds go by. My sister's friends were always there. But we were suddenly aware, in the same manner a date palm seems to suddenly sprout fruit, girls were everywhere and we wanted nothing more than to be around them.

Twenty-Three
A poem about losing my virginity.

After

Twenty-Four
Virginity is defined as "the state or condition of being pure, fresh, or unused." Why is the experience of one's sexuality besmirch this condition? Why does it mean something so different for a woman to "lose" hers than a man? This poem reflects on that from a young mind.

Twenty-Five
As a boy, I was taught to be "hard," to fight, to be first, and to be strongest. This is a poem about how when a man is broken, it is the woman's words that raise him. Strength beyond strength.

Twenty-Six

A poem about dating outside of my race. In the American South interracial dating retains, even to this day, a stigma. I felt it throughout my teenage years and into adulthood.

Thirty

My cousin Zephyr drowned in the bay near our home. This poem is dedicated to her.

Thirty-Two

This poem is not solely about staying in the room or staying in a relationship, but staying in tune with your integrity as a human. About taking care with and responsibility for your actions.

Thirty-Four

The first time I learned about periods I was awed. What power… what magic… what a remarkable thing in this world for a body to be capable of accomplishing.

Thirty-Six

My mother defined beauty to me, as I am sure is the case with all little boys. But, my mother, a strong Black woman, never had her likeness associated with popular concepts of beauty. To live your life—my sisters, my cousins, my daughter—and so rarely see your likeness defined as "beautiful" is a horrifying reality of our world. This poem reflects on that.

Thirty-Seven

A poem on a sex lesson from an older woman.

Thirty-Eight

Growing up, popular culture rarely portrayed black men worthy of love—of men heroic, steady, kind, friendly, or any of the attributes regularly associated with men in romantic films and stories.

Forty
I was married. This is a poem about separating from my wife.

Forty-Seven
A man carries every day of his life with him. He learns to love with it, builds his life with it, and raises his kids with it.

Forty-Eight
When I was 23, I made the biggest mistake of my life. This poem reflects on that.

Forty-Nine
Love isn't about finding someone, but about finding oneself. You must go beyond your comfort and find you. Fall in love with you.

Fifty-One
For my daughter, Ella.

Fifty-Four
A poem reflecting the many assignments to the body and the image we are taught to have of our own.

Woman

Fifty-Eight
This is a poem about trusting the lessons taught to you.

Sixty-One
I had a thought about water, and how it represents

the woman. It cannot be owned, claimed, or have its power diminished. Man is land. While they are opposite, appreciation and support keep balance. In a world absurdly disproportionate to the patriarchy, balance is more needed now than ever.

Sixty-Three

A teacher of mine, who shall remain nameless, said "What if more little boys pretended to be their mothers" and it always stuck with me. Indeed, what would that world look like?

Sixty-Five

Beauty grows with age and with wisdom. The era in which we live, where youth is idolized to the edge of perversion, in doing so blinds us all. This poem reflects on the lie of youth and the beauty of age.

Sixty-Eight

The only thing you can give another worth giving is freedom. And that isn't yours to give.

Seventy-Five

While this book is conversations with women, it is to say, the *feminine spirit*; capable, I believe, of existing in all persons. Gender, then, is just a construct; one we've learned to accept and to weaponize; the first crack in a fractured world. We, all of us and at all times, carry the spirit of the masculine and the feminine.

Seventy-Six

A poem about abortion.

Seventy-Eight

A poem about finding my soulmate.

Eighty-Three

Black woman, there is so much to say about you and so much that need be said. This poem is mostly a calling. We need you more now than ever.

Eighty-Six

A poem about sex as not a goal ending in orgasm, but a connection as old and as fundamental as breathing.

Eighty-Eight

Too many men stand in the army of patriarchy. Woman, you are strong enough to fight, clever enough to strategize, and bold enough to change the world without the help of a man. All I can offer you, is to not stand in your way.

Cebo Campbell is an author and creative director based in Brooklyn, New York. Winner of the Linda B. Ross Creative Writing Award and the Stories Award for Poetry, Cebo's work has been featured in numerous publications. Cebo is the co-founder of the award-winning creative agency, Spherical, where he leads a team of creatives in shaping the best hotel brands in the world.

His debut novel, *All the Qualities of Soil* is due out in 2022.

Cebo Campbell's *Violet in Some Places* is the recipient of the 2019 Stories Award for Poetry, an annual submission competition for full-length poetry titles by a single author, sponsored by Stories Books & Cafe in Echo Park, Los Angeles.

For more information, please visit **www.notacult.media.**

CPSIA information can be obtained
at www.ICGtesting.com
Printed in the USA
JSHW031542220821
18061JS00002B/6